Inspirations
Preston Bailey

Inspirations

Preston Bailey

PHOTOGRAPHY BY JOHN LABBÉ

Bulfinch Press
New York • Boston

Bulfinch Press

Hachette Book Group USA
1271 Avenue of the Americas, New York, NY 10020
Visit our Web site at www.bulfinchpress.com

First Edition: November 2006

Library of Congress Cataloging-in-Publication Data
Bailey, Preston.
  Inspirations / Preston Bailey.
      p. cm.
  Includes index.
  ISBN-10: 0-8212-5817-6 (hardcover)
  ISBN-13: 978-0-8212-5817-0 (hardcover)
  1.   Party decorations. 2.   Parties—Planning.   I. Title.
TT900.P3B35 2006
642'.4—dc22   2006004118

Designed by Doug Turshen with David Huang

PRINTED IN SINGAPORE

*To all of my colleagues and associates
who continue to inspire me
every day — I dedicate this book to you
and thank you for your hard work,
support, and friendship.*

Introduction

SOMETIMES IT'S AS EASY AS TAKING A BREATH.

Inspiration can come from anywhere. It can come at any time. It can come quickly, like a flash of lightning; it can come slowly, like a gathering storm. It can, quite possibly, not come at all. Or it can come when you're not looking for it. The key, therefore, is to keep your eyes open, your antennae up, your senses attuned to the endlessly provocative world at your periphery. Blink, and you might miss it. Hold your breath…and the moment will pass you by.

My work, essentially, is about inspiration. It involves a great deal of hard work, to be sure, but everything begins with the *idea*—that mysterious, elusive, and unpredictable commodity. As I said, there are times an idea can enter your body on a breeze, as effortless as inhaling. Other times, it must be laboriously coaxed out, a difficult birth, a painstaking solution. I must say I prefer the former. The latter is rather like doing math. And I never was all that good at math.

Admittedly, I didn't have much patience for school. There was something about being cooped up indoors that my spirit just couldn't abide. I wanted to be outside—in the forests, the ocean, the open air. Academics, I'm afraid, never inspired much passion in me.

Which, of course, is not to say that passions weren't present. I am nothing if not an avid learner and a curious soul. It's just that my style of study is more of the autodidactic variety. When a subject piques my interest, I want to discover everything about it, immersing myself in the pursuit and voraciously digesting whatever I can get my hands (and eyes) on. Nature was always such a source of wonder. People as well. Those two endlessly fertile and inextinguishably surprising fonts of fascination have been the wellsprings to which I've returned time and time again in my career.

More often than not, my fabulous clients—many of whom you'll meet in this book—have been the inspiration for the ideas that bloom into the flowers of my design. In planning any event, a salient part of my process is to sit with the clients and get to know them. And, to put it bluntly, get into their heads. I strive to unlock their storehouse of fantasies. I want to get a glimpse of their dreams. Once I've gleaned a sense of their imagination, my work can become a form of *inhabitation.* In a way, it's almost what I imagine an actor's process to be like. A kind of getting-into-character, or mimicry. I've always been a bit of a mimic, really—taking the people I most admire and copying their best habits. Discipline can be accomplished in that way.

And it may appear paradoxical, but discipline is instrumental in the capturing of inspiration. That moment of epiphany—the "divine intervention"—will come only once the homework, legwork, and groundwork have been done. Once one's art, skill, and craft are well honed and well applied, I truly believe it's only a matter of *respiration.* Whether you're motionless, meditating, incubating, letting the mind percolate…or on the move, exercising, running, letting the endorphins stimulate…it's all a matter of letting the air in. Fill your lungs. Fill your heart.

Breathe in…

Contemporary Conservatory in Texas

I'VE ALWAYS BEEN PARTIAL TO CONSERVATORIES. There's something magical about these crystalline creations—bright, airy retreats from the workaday life, bulwarks against the impassive changing of the seasons.

With the proliferation of glass roofs in the nineteenth century, plain masonry structures originally intended for housing delicate plants quickly evolved into elaborate edifices, erected more for recreational than botanical pursuits. Built as an extension to the main house, a private conservatory conferred instant status upon its owner and provided the perfect setting for year-round entertainment.

When I was asked by a prominent Texas family to take the reins of an event to be held at a private club, a crystal annex was the first image that leaped to mind. There was to be a tent raised on the club's property, but the question remained: How do we transform a canvas covering into a glass superstructure? We'll get to that in a moment.

It was important to the host that a prominent visual flourish would signal the delights to come before the guests entered the club, so we used the tall windows of the façade to create a welcoming, festive effect. The host was also very specific about color, favoring a variety of coral tones, so we lit the room from within and suspended alternating strings of rose globes (containing at least two dozen flowers) and spheroids made of foam, hanging in each window like a bubble curtain. For the entrance, I procured a cluster of unique

"Midsummer Light" lampshades produced by designer Tord Boontje, whose installation I had seen recently at the Victoria and Albert Museum in London. The floral-inspired shades cast a lovely coral blush on the invitees as they made their way into the club for the cocktail reception.

Once inside, they passed through an anteroom decorated with trompe l'oeil wall hangings and a sundial adorned with radiating roses. A collection of ice sculptures, each with architectural details in the style of Lalique vases, held the centerpieces. When the guests were summoned for dinner and left the space, the same room was quickly converted into a lounge for the after-party, with a dance floor and neon-accented lighting.

Another European experience from which I derived a spark of inspiration was a floral exhibit I'd seen in the streets of Paris, in which an entire city block had been completely blanketed with flowers. I adapted that idea to the outdoor grounds of the club. We measured out a series of squares using wood partitions and filled them in with sod and thousands of fresh flowers—red, yellow, pink, and orange roses.

Finally, the conservatory. We constructed an endo- and exoskeleton of Plexiglas both inside and outside the tent (incidentally, the tent itself was still necessary, because neither structure was actually functional, i.e., weather-proof). Inside, the palette was concentrated in whites, creams, and pale greens, and there were petite pools dappled with floating phalaenopsis orchids. Frosted glass fixtures emitting a gentle light hovered above the dining room, and white birch trees provided the foundation for a set of six-foot topiaries of various designs, arising gracefully from the tables.

Dining and dancing in this glowing ballroom conservatory, the convocation easily could have been mistaken for a klatch of revelers at a fin-de-siècle court entertainment, oblivious to the passage of time outside their crystal arcadia.

A detail from a trompe l'oeil wall hanging—red berry beads commingle with thousands of bunched flower petals. (Opposite) In a stroke of brilliance, Jill Fortuny (an invaluable party planner) suggested this "candy bar" at the exit. Just as we've seen the benefits of bestowing little keepsakes or trinkets on the guests at their place settings, a farewell sweet as they depart is a note of hospitality. A mouthwatering selection of pink, orange, yellow, and coral candy was the perfect send-off.

Autumnal Artistry
in Virginia

I WAS BORN AND RAISED IN PANAMA. It is a beautiful country, abundant with natural wonders from border to border. I grew up loving the rain forests. I was in awe of their spectacular lushness, and I discovered a new kind of spirituality under their canopies. My family went to church regularly, but it was there, surrounded by the soaring trees, that I was made fully aware of the presence of a higher power. The experience instilled in me a conviction that I have carried in my heart the rest of my life: that we create our own church wherever we are. And for me, a natural setting is a place of worship.

I immigrated to America in 1969, and I still vividly remember my first autumn in the United States. Seasons were a revelation to me. In Panama, there are only two seasons: rainy and dry. I wasn't prepared for the exquisite explosion of North American fall foliage. Especially after a rainfall, the glittering leaves of maples, oaks, and elms took my breath away. I had found yet more natural wonders to be inspired by.

So when my client, Dr. Johnson, asked me to design her wedding and suggested that we run with a fall theme, I was thrilled by the opportunity to conceive my own vision of autumn. Since the wedding was planned for September—not exactly peak season—and was to be held on the Johnsons' Virginia estate, certain liberties needed to be taken.

Foremost was the issue of where to perform the ceremony. It was important to Dr. Johnson that the wedding take place in a church.

With necessity being the mother of invention, I offered to build a church for them, creating a clapboard façade and transforming the capacious stable into an intimate chapel. For the interior, however, Dr. Johnson and I decided to bring nature indoors and fill the "pews" with dozens of handmade trees. We draped thousands of silk leaves in glorious fall colors on the branches and then arranged a constellation of votive candles that led the bride toward an elegant altar framed by a scrim of transparent foliage. A natural church, if there ever was one, with a woodland illusion that could give my beloved rain forest a run for its money.

For the reception, I took the adjacent riding arena and refashioned it as an homage to the Great Palace in Moscow, mimicking the imperial residence's intricately carved woodwork with decorative oaken columns supporting the vaulted, billowing ceilings. The botanical panels lining the tsar's ornate corridors were reimagined as trompe l'oeil wall hangings. For good measure, we added Balinese-inspired floral chandeliers, suspended from above. The cumulative effect was certainly a departure from the ceremonial Americana of the chapelized stable, but I loved the subtle frisson between the two locations. North American, Russian, and Indonesian influences all collided unexpectedly to produce a singular, completely original effect.

And—as a final, bountiful touch—we constructed two ten-foot pineapples out of sunflowers (the happiest flower, I think) and palm fronds. In addition to being one of my favorite fruits, the pineapple is a symbol of hospitality and good fortune. It may not be a staple of the traditional colonial harvest, but a little blending of cultures in the service of festivity is always welcome, in my opinion.

Our intricately designed tent was also inspired by the Great Palace in Moscow.
To mimic the paneling on the ceiling, we created architectural patterns with fabric.
Also, the entire structure needed to be fireproof, which we achieved without
sacrificing any aesthetic integrity. (Opposite) I got the idea for this circular chandelier
from a visit I took to a mosque. It's another of our custom designs,
conceived and built entirely in-house.

With this series of images from the reception, you can really get a sense of how deep
into pink we went with the details. (Left to right) After the jewelry box allusion in our ceremonial
chuppah, we decided to get a little more literal with the place settings, incorporating
a heart-shaped keepsake into the layout. Each souvenir was filled with special candies, each heart's
contents different from the rest. Sometimes we get fancy with the napkin-folding.
Here, four roses are attached to the corners for some extra flair. A close-up of a place setting.

open-air tent for the cocktail party and dinner.

The tent brings up an essential point for any al fresco event: it is important always to have a fallback option. My good friend and collaborator Marcy Blum, who planned the wedding, always says, "Never, ever, under any circumstance, create an outdoor scenario without a backup plan!" Luckily, the weather cooperated, but the tent was still an invaluable asset. With the river in the background, it reminded me of a white-sailed clipper.

Lined along the centers of the tables were curvaceous glass sculptures which I thought subtly captured the rolling waves of water. Not only were they wonderfully sensuous objets d'art, but they were also quite protean in their applications. For example, after the beautiful sunset, they gained practical use as evening lights, casting a warm glow on the repast.

The glass sculptures also fit nicely into my design for the table arrangement. I'd been studying the layout of seventeenth-century French gardens and thought of casting the place settings in their highly symmetrical style. Intricately laced leis of tiny orchids became the divisionary *parterres de broderie,* with cubed votive candles as flickering pools. In this context, the glass sculptures functioned as fanciful topiaries, a vertical complement to the ordered horizontal plane of the "garden."

As a final transformative touch, we converted the elegant daytime cocktail patio into a sexy nocturnal pasha's den. For the cocktail hour, the slate deck was tastefully draped in pure white, punctuated only by the deep incarnadine hues of cherries, plums, and champagne grapes. When the sun went down, we stripped the white covers from the furniture and unleashed the colors. A cluster of green apple lamps dangled above the dance floor, in contrast to the wash of orange projected onto the convex bend of the tent's ceiling. It was as if we'd captured a downtown nightclub and brought it up to Niagara with us. It was a flash of urbanity in the midst of a divine pastoral scene.

Star-Studded Cabaret at the Pierre

REMEMBER WHAT THE MASTER OF CEREMONIES says at the beginning of *Cabaret*? "Leave your troubles outside…here, life is beautiful!" Though his context is considerably different, the MC's precept is something I strive to achieve in every aspect of my work. When a guest walks through the door, he or she should be immediately transported. The quotidian reality of the outside world vanishes, and a fantasy land takes its place. My task, principally, is to make life beautiful.

Speaking of musical theater, I've noticed a trend of late in my profession: injecting a glamorous dose of entertainment into the proceedings. Personally, I love it when performances are included. My designs are undeniably theatrical, so it makes sense for there to be bursts of actual song and dance. For example, at the Four Seasons event described elsewhere in this book, music phenomena Michael Feinstein and Marvin Hamlisch both made appearances. In fact, they so enjoyed an impromptu duet that they later discussed touring together.

Theatrical is a perfect word to describe a reception I put together for the irreplaceable, irrepressible Regis Philbin at the Pierre Hotel in New York. In honor of his daughter J.J.'s nuptials, it was one of the most talked-about society events of the year. A particular challenge I faced was how to strike a balance between the eclectic tastes of J.J. and the more traditional preferences of her parents. Regis's fabulous wife, Joy, turned out to be of great assistance in this department. Like me, she adores flowers, and she helped me select a palette that shifted between conservative coloration and more rambunctious hues.

First, for the cocktail hour, we went with a mise-en-scène of whites, creams, and celadons. The room faced Central Park, and I wanted to give the interior a hint of the exterior, so we placed a few of our handmade birch trees at center stage and mingled voluptuous orchids with the leaves. The trees stood in close proximity to the most playful invention of the evening. I'd been toying with the idea of creating a huge cake for the event, but I hadn't settled on how to carry it off. A colleague of mine, Ron Fenstermacher, an excellent interior designer, casually suggested that we erect a "cake bar." And that's exactly what we did, arranging the bottles and glasses around a towering three-tiered "cake."

Inside the ballroom, we opted for a "starry night" theme, with an explosion of galvanic color. Projections of five-pointed stars covered the ceiling, and lines of crystal beads hung from halos of roses to enhance the stellar composition. For the lighting, I wanted a kinetic mélange of pink, blue, and magenta—colors that reminded me of the bright nebulae I'd seen in photographs of the Milky Way. The floral table arrangements also complemented the galactic spectrum, with roses and orchids resonating in a volcanic flush of corals, pinks, and oranges.

Before the evening was through, Neil Sedaka dazzled the audience with a swinging set, and the one and only Tony Bennett was truly the icing on the cake, singing a surprise serenade to the blushing bride.

The *actual* cake was a fairly dramatic confection in itself, a delightfully asymmetrical affair not unlike a bright pink Leaning Tower of Pisa, confected by the extraordinary Sylvia Weinstock.